Jock Tamson's Bairns
*A history of the records of the
General Register Office for Scotland*

Cecil Sinclair

EDINBURGH:
GENERAL REGISTER OFFICE FOR SCOTLAND

© Crown Copyright 2000

First published 2000

British Library Cataloguing in Publication Data.
A catalogue record for this book is available from the British Library

ISBN 1 874451 59 1

Acknowledgements:
Registrar General for Scotland; National Museums of Scotland
(Scottish Life Archive); National Gallery of Scotland;
National Archives of Scotland;
Glasgow Museums and Art Galleries; Aberdeen Art Gallery and Museums.

Illustrations: Front Cover - (clockwise from top left)
New Register House Dome ceiling
Old Parochial Registers in New Register House
Dome stacks in New Register House
Maid at Sanna, Ardnamurchan 1925
(Scottish Life Archive)
Statutory birth entry for Arthur Conan Doyle and handbills
(GROS Collection)
Shipyard workers on Steamship "Lusitania", Clydeside 1907
(reproduced with kind permission of the Keeper of the Records of Scotland).

Back Cover - (from top)
Death register volumes in New Register House
Funeral establishment, Peat Neuk Close, Leith - (Scottish Life Archive)
Ornamental gateway, New Register House.

Research: Bruno Longmore, Departmental Record Officer, GROS
Helen Borthwick, Librarian, GROS
Printing: David Winter & Son Ltd, Dundee
Design: Mandy Witty

For more information, see websites
http://www.gro-scotland.gov.uk
http://www.origins.net

Preface

Tracing family history is becoming more and more popular all over the world. It is a subject of absorbing interest, providing a personal link with the past.

In New Register House in Edinburgh, we hold three major sets of historical records which are invaluable to all Scots, and those of Scottish descent, who wish to undertake ancestry or local history research. A chapter of this book is devoted to each. Thousands of people from all parts of the globe consult these records every year ~ by personal visits to Edinburgh, postal enquiries, or over the Internet.

The aim of the book is to describe the main records, and to set them in their historical context. Along the way, attention is drawn to some of the quirks of the records, using actual examples and some excellent illustrations which bring the documents to life.

Cecil Sinclair has produced an entertaining and very readable account. As the title of the book suggests, our heritage is not just to do with the famous or the unusual. I hope this book will be of interest not only to experienced genealogists but also to a wide cross-section of the general public who value their personal and social heritage and wish to learn more about it.

J N RANDALL
Registrar General
April 2000

Introduction

The post of Registrar General for Scotland was created by an Act of Parliament in 1854. This Act and the 1920 Census Act provided him with the three main functions: to establish, maintain and supervise a compulsory system of registration of all births, deaths and marriages within Scotland (commencing in 1855); to gather in and preserve the old parochial registers, in which were recorded baptisms, marriages and burials until 1854; and to supervise the undertaking of the decennial census of the country.

This little book looks at the three categories of record, generated by these functions and held by the Registrar General, from an historical viewpoint. It is hoped that the discussion in this book will raise awareness among its readers of the character and context of these records by describing their history, content and value to researchers, whether these are family, local or social historians.

Because this is an historical publication, the chapter on the censuses concentrates on the 19th century census records, which are open to the public. Similarly, the chapter on the statutory registers of birth, death and marriage mainly describes the early history of these records, though edging into the 20th century.

All three sets of records are preserved and may be consulted in Edinburgh in New Register House, which was built between 1859 and 1863 to house the General Register Office for Scotland, the government department headed by the Registrar General. While the census records are open to researchers only after one hundred years, there is no time bar on public access to the old parochial registers or the post-1854 statutory registers.

Research for this publication was done largely in these records themselves and in the records created by the work of the Registrar General's Department. The historical files of that department are now preserved by the National Archives of Scotland and may be consulted in West Register House.

New Register House, Edinburgh. Designed by Robert Matheson and built between 1859-1863 to house the records of Scottish civil registration. It remains the headquarters of the General Register Office for Scotland to this day.

The Old Parochial Registers

Birth and death are the two unavoidable events of human life. For many people, marriage comes as a significant third. Humankind usually seeks to celebrate these events, and for the Christian Church, they are the grounds of the sacraments of baptism of the new born and of marriage, and the rite of the burial of the dead.

Since written records began, the births, deaths and marriages of princes and some other great people have been recorded, but for centuries those of lesser folk were mostly unrecorded. We died to be forgotten. Admittedly, the Old Testament lists genealogies of the Jewish people of that time, and there are reports of such records being gathered in Greek and Roman times and in medieval France and Italy. But if any such records were compiled in Scotland before the mid-16th century, they have not survived. In post-medieval Europe, the first serious attempt at registration was enacted in Spain in 1497. Organised by parish, the motivation was to ensure that marriages were not within the prohibited degrees. In England, registration was begun by an Act in 1538, requiring every parson to maintain a register in which to record every wedding, christening and burial within his parish.

Both in Scotland and in England, the parish was the administrative area of government closest to daily lives of the people. Civil and ecclesiastical in character, it existed not only to regulate religious observances and moral behaviour but also to provide education and poor relief. Because of its small size and the familiarity of its presiding clergyman with its inhabitants, it provided the best location within which to keep registers of what are today sometimes known as "hatches, matches and despatches".

In Scotland, there were a series of enactments by both Church and State to establish parish registers during the times of religious change in the later 16th and 17th centuries. In 1552, a provincial council of the Roman

The earliest surviving Scottish old parish register is for Errol in Perthshire. The first baptism recorded is for a baby girl, Christane or Christine Hay, baptised 27 December 1553. The record dates from pre-Reformation Scotland. (OPR351/1)

Catholic Scottish clergy ordained that every parish should keep a register of baptisms and a register of proclamations of marriage. In 1565, a Protestant General Assembly of the Church of Scotland instructed every minister, once they had been provided with a manse and glebe, to keep a register of persons deceased in their parish. Though the earliest surviving register, that of the parish of Errol, dates from 1553, the number of subsequent instructions from both Church and State authorities, along with our knowledge of the registers which survive throughout the country, show that in many parts of Scotland, registration was slow to catch on.

Now, why was registration of baptisms, marriages and deaths so important? The Kirk was responsible for the moral welfare of its parishioners and by baptism and marriage ceremonies sought to have control over them. Also, a child who had a recognised father was the responsibility of that father and would not be a financial burden on the parish. But the more important reasons were legal. The attempt to register deaths in 1565 was in order "that pupils [children] and creditors be not defrauded", in other words to ensure that the wealth of the dead person went to those entitled to it. Registration meant publicity and, it was hoped, reliability. In 1616, the Scottish Government, by an Act of the Privy Council, ordered that a register be kept in every parish of persons married, baptised or deceased, because diverse questions often arose in the law courts which depended on accurate information of the times of marriages, baptisms and decease of persons. It was fondly hoped that such a register would provide conclusive proof in family disputes, usually over inheritance.

Unfortunately, the keeping of these registers over the next two hundred years was not as satisfactory or reliable as the Privy Council had intended. The minister of Hawick in the 1790s admitted "There is no exact register kept of marriages, baptisms or burials" and lots of other ministers confessed that their parish registers were "imperfectly kept". While it is not always clear whether absent records have gone astray or were never compiled in the first place, it is apparent that the surviving records of the more remote parishes tend to start very late, at the end of the 18th century or even in the 19th. The Western Isles are particularly badly served. Even where the records of a parish started earlier, few of the series are in any way complete.

Assuming that they were created in the first place, why is it that so many volumes of this valuable record have not survived? It should be remembered that the parish registers were the responsibility of the parish minister and kirk session. They were compiled either by the minister or the session clerk who was usually the local schoolmaster. The register volumes and notes from which the volumes were to be compiled would be kept in the manse or the schoolmaster's house. Both men would have had other important commitments. Let us now consider probable reasons why these important records so often have disappeared.

(1) Fire. If the manse or the schoolmaster's house caught fire, then any registers therein would probably burn too. In the days of wood or coal or peat fires and of candles there was always a fire risk. In the parish of Muthill, a register for 1704 to 1760 had to be compiled from peoples' memories or their jottings "the original Registers of that time having been burnt in the Session-Clerk's house with several things of his own". (OPR386a/1)

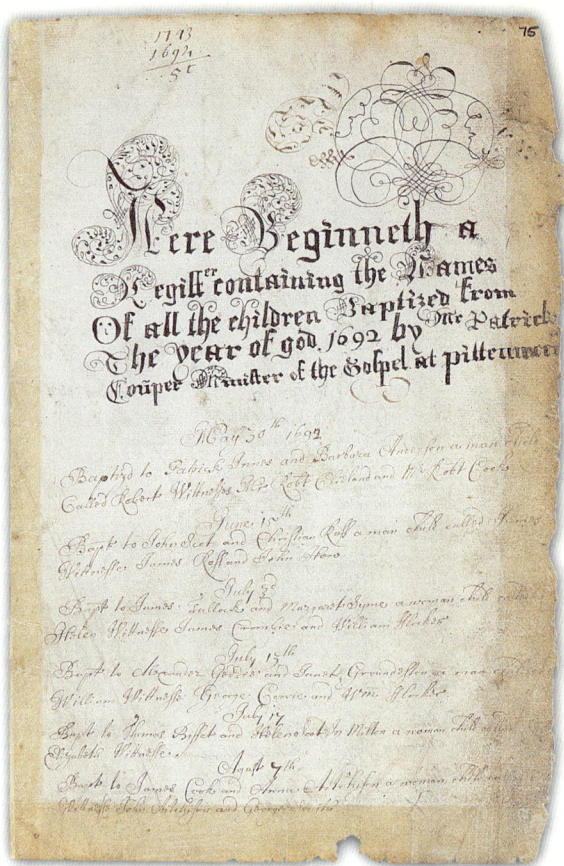

Illustration from the baptism register for the parish of Pittenweem in Fife as recorded by the minister Patrick Couper from 1692. (OPR452/1)

(2) Water. A register of the parish of Abertarff was lost when accidentally dropped into a rapid stream, which the custodian was crossing. But a more common fate was for the paper volumes to moulder away through being kept in damp attics or cellars or out-houses.

(3) Rodents. Volumes stored away and not consulted regularly were ideal fodder for hungry mice.

(4) Borrowing. As one of the purposes of keeping such registers was to provide evidence in courts of law, it is hardly surprising that registers were borrowed for that purpose. Unfortunately, once borrowed, there was no certainty that a register would be returned, instead hiding in a lawyer's office, whether locally or in Edinburgh.

(5) Removed. A minister or session clerk, moving to another parish might inadvertently or wilfully take a register with him. When in 1690, the minister

of Carriden was deposed for drunkenness, he allegedly took away the parochial records. Similarly, the family of a deceased minister might bundle up the registers with his other possessions and walk off with them.

(6) Destroyed accidentally. The earliest registers of Yetholm were reportedly "destroyed accidentally by the family of one of the former ministers of the parish." Spring cleaning has a lot to answer for!

(7) Destroyed deliberately. While one hopes that deliberate destruction was extremely rare, in the parish of Castleton in Roxburghshire in January 1649, soldiers of the invading English army carried away the records of baptisms and marriages and used them to light their tobacco pipes.

(8) Confusion with other records. No pro-forma volumes were issued for the purpose of the parochial registers. Consequently, session clerks tended to record baptisms, marriages and burials in volumes also used for other purposes. Such records were commonly written in with the kirk session minutes or accounts, and might even be in the same volumes as someone's private or business accounts. In 1855 the registrar of Laggan reported that "entries of Births, Deaths and Marriages are intermixed with entries of records relating to sessional and other matters in the most hopeless state of confusion". Thus, these books might not always be recognised as parochial registers.

However, not all the history of these missing records is tragic. Some may be remarkably recovered. A register of the parish of Kirkden, 1650-1690, after having been lost for a long while, was discovered by an 18th century minister when one of the leaves was casually sent from a shop in the neighbourhood, presumably as wrapping paper. Those which have gone astray and not been destroyed may still be found, and, even well into the 20th century, such wanderers have been traced and recovered by the Registrar General. Sometimes, they have been kept by the local minister or session clerk (usually confused with the kirk session records) or even the local registrar years after they should have been brought into the Registrar General's custody. A portion of the OPR for Firth and Stenness 1732-1745, in the possession of that kirk session, came to public knowledge through an article in the Scotsman. The register for the parish of Tomintoul 1827-1846 had been kept by the minister's family in the belief that it was a private record. A duplicate record of the parish of Knockando 1768-91 was found "in an old garret in Elgin". A Coldingham register was discovered in a desk purchased by an antique dealer. Some have turned up in sale-rooms as far away as London. Others have been revealed when sought by a claimant to an old-age pension born before 1855. Quite recently, a register for Inverkeithing 1710-1744, long thought lost, was discovered among Court of Session records in the National Archives.

The imperfect condition of the Old Parochial Registers has been long known. In 1779, Arnot's History of Edinburgh was very rude about the keeping of the Edinburgh registers. The Statistical Account of Scotland published between 1791 and 1795 and The New Statistical Account published in 1845, both consisting of reports on each parish in the country by the parish minister, are full of comments on the unsatisfactory nature of the parish registers. (Some of these comments are quoted in this work.) In 1816, the topic was discussed by the General Assembly. In 1854, arguing for a system of compulsory registration, George Seton published his influential Sketch of the History and Imperfect Condition of the Parochial Records of Births, Deaths and Marriages in Scotland, demonstrating the faults of the then system.

The faults were not just in the absence of many volumes of registers. The faults were also in how the surviving registers had been kept. Little guidance had been given to the ministers and session clerks who compiled the registers and they were left to their own devices, resulting in a marked lack of consistency between and within parishes. Note also that there was no compulsion on individuals to register their family events. So now let us look at the imperfections of the surviving registers, and the causes thereof, real or alleged. But firstly, it is important to realise that generally it was not births as such that were supposed to be recorded but baptisms, not marriages but the proclamations of banns of marriage, and not deaths but burials.

(1) Money. The session clerk might expect a tip. The Kirk charged for making proclamations of banns (the money went to the poor). Not everyone could afford to pay. Worse still, an Act of 1783 put a tax of 3d on every registration, an Act later repealed in 1794, but not before damage had been done in people avoiding registration. For many people, three pence could be better spent. In Fala and Soutra, it was complained that no accurate register was kept, "owing partly to the negligence of the recorder, and partly to the parsimony of the inhabitants, who do not chuse to pay the trifling fees of registration".

(2) Dissenters or non-conformists. Not everyone was a member of the established Church of Scotland. In some parts of the country, the Church of Rome still had a substantial following. Similarly, even after the Church of Scotland became firmly Presbyterian, many people remained Episcopalian. But most troublesome of all was the tendency of Presbyterian believers to split off from the established church, on points of principle, and set up their own church. The most famous of these divisions was the Disruption of 1843, but that

was only the latest of a long series. Though the established minister of the parish was supposed to include all parishioners in the registers, many of the dissenters refused to provide him with the necessary information, fearing contagion if they did. Some ministers entered the baptisms etc. only of their own flock, some made an effort to include those of the other denominations. There is no consistency on this in the Old Parochial Registers. Fortunately, some of the dissenting churches kept their own record of baptisms, marriages and burials, though these were as irregularly kept as the official registers. Many of these records of other churches are preserved and may be consulted in the National Archives of Scotland.

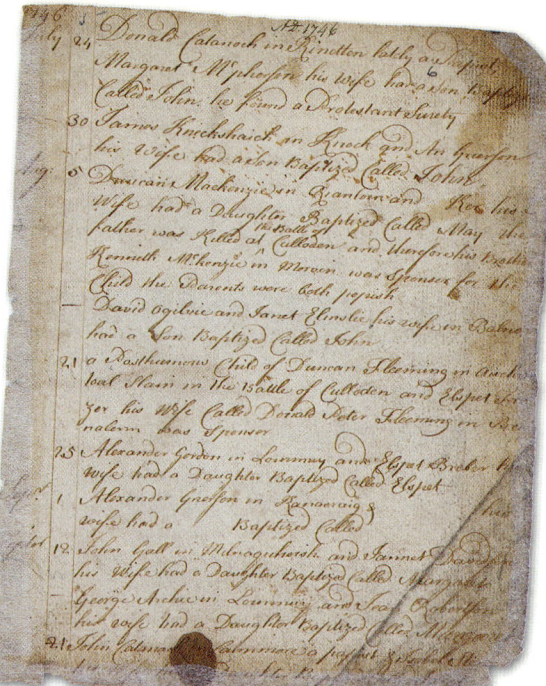

Baptisms in 1746 from Glenmuick, Tullich and Glengairn in Aberdeen-shire, for children born to men who had died at the battle of Culloden. The baptism entry for Duncan Mackenzie's child records that the family were Catholics, "..the Parents were both popish". (OPR201/1)

(3) Irregular marriages. Before 1940, there were three forms of irregular marriage in Scotland. (a) Marriage by habit and repute, where a couple simply set up house together and were regarded by their families and neighbours, over a period of time, as man and wife. This form of irregular marriage is still technically legal, so bidey-ins, beware! (b) When a man promised marriage to a woman, then got her pregnant, that could make them legally married. (c) When a man and woman declared before witnesses that they were man and wife, that was a marriage. Many dissenters who were married by their own clergyman took this path. It was the type of marriage made famous at Gretna. Obviously in all these cases, there were no banns of marriage and, therefore, except where some dissenting marriages were noted, likely to be no record in the parish registers. In the 1790s, the minister of Eccles, explaining the small number of registered marriages in his parish, remarked "that the practice of marrying in a clandestine and irregular manner still subsists upon the Borders". The point of the law allowing such marriages was to render any children legitimate, which gave them rights of inheritance.

(4) Unworthiness of parents. If a child was a product of pre-marital fornication (a remarkably common occurrence), then baptism might only proceed after the parents had done public penance and expressed contrition for their sin. This would also happen if the father was guilty of any other offence in the eyes of the kirk session. An unbaptised child was not recorded, which would obviously also occur if an infant child died before baptism.

(5) Mortcloths. A mortcloth was a cloth which covered the coffin at a funeral. Each kirk session kept one or more mortcloths to be rented out

Scotland's most famous irregular marriage between Robert Burns and Joan (or Jean) Armour, Mauchline, Ayrshire, 1788. The church took a dim view of such unorthodox arrangements as recorded by the entry, "..the session rebuked both parties for this irregularity and took them solemnly bound to adhere to one another as husband & wife all the days of their life". (OPR604/2)

for use at parish burials. The record of burials in many parishes is simply the record of the letting out of the mortcloth, so that if the kirk's mortcloth was not used on any occasion, no record was made of that burial. This might occur because the deceased or his family were too poor, when either no mortcloth would be used or no charge made. In Coldstream, "the poor who were buried at the public expense were not taken notice of except occasionally". No record of the burial might exist because a family had its own mortcloth and therefore did not use the parish one. Also, if a local landowner had gifted the mortcloth to the parish, that family would not be charged for the use of it, and therefore again no record.

(6) Deaths and burials outside the parish. Those who were lost at sea were not buried in the kirkyard and consequently their deaths would usually be unrecorded. Those who died on land but away from home might be buried in a foreign parish. It was also quite common for the remains of those whose families had come from another parish to be taken for burial in that parish. In Peterculter, "The number of dead brought hither for interment, from Aberdeen and its neighbourhood, exceeds the number of persons who die within the parish". For this reason, the register of burials of the parish of Grange was kept only for four years then given up "as it appeared that the burials did not correspond at all with the deaths".

(7) Alcohol. Arnot in 1779 accused the Edinburgh burial registrars of drunkenness, and thereby incapable of compiling the register accurately. Certainly the ceremonies of baptism, marriage and funeral were usually accompanied by a party in which strong drink was taken. It is easy to imagine the circumstances in which notes of proceedings were lost, or in which wrong information was entered in the register, or the register itself mislaid.

Too good a party after the ceremony? Clearly whoever wrote this entry in 1704 forgot who had been baptised ~ "George Something lawful son to What-ye-call-him". (OPR609/1)

(8) Carelessness. Some registers were kept in loose leaf form, which made them more vulnerable than those kept in volumes. Notes of events might not be transcribed into the register volume. There are gaps in some registers which can only be explained by a minister or session clerk failing to fulfil his duty to make entries in the register. Within a register, baptisms, marriages and other unrelated matters might be entered higgledy-piggledy (or "promiscuously" as Seton put it) regardless of date order or sense. There might even be incorrect entries (perish the thought!). Since 1855, the Registrar General has had the power to correct entries in the OPRs. Individuals have first to petition the sheriff, complaining, for example, that a name was "John" not "James" or "Wright" not "Wight".

(9) Legibility. The pre-1700 registers were kept in a script with letter forms unfamiliar to us, but that can be resolved by learning the letter forms, which is not difficult. More serious is the problem of plain bad writing, whatever century. Ink, perhaps watered down to save money, has faded. Ink on one side of a page has soaked through to the other, rendering both sides of the page difficult to read. "The paper is much worn and the writing in places has become faded and indistinct" described the register of baptisms and

marriages for the parish of South Ronaldsay 1657-69, but can also describe many other of the older registers. These problems may be accentuated when a register is viewed on microfilm.

The weaknesses and limitations of the Old Parochial Registers have been well aired and it is sad that so much information is not included in them. Yet much information may be found in these invaluable volumes. Most of us who look in them find some ancestors, while the lucky ones of us may find many generations and their kinsfolk. So let us now consider what information is or may be contained in these registers of baptisms, proclamations of marriage, and burials.

As already said, do not expect consistency. Generally speaking, the earlier registers have the less information and the later volumes provide the more. It can be very frustrating for researchers to be presented just with names and little or no further information. There was a rather small pool of Christian names, and in many parishes an even smaller pool of surnames. Spelling, including of Christian names, surnames and place-names is not fixed as it is today. Names are spelled as the minister or session clerk writing them chose to spell them. Thus one man in his lifetime could be called Robertson or Robson or Robison or Robeson and probably other variants. These variations were not the result of carelessness. It was just that exact spelling was not regarded as important.

Baptisms

Though the record was of baptisms, quite often the date of birth is also given. Thus, we are told that George, son of George Robertson in Grutha, South Ronaldsay, baptised on the 25 September 1831, was born on 4 September 1831, the day his parents married! (OPR29/4)

Particularly in the early registers, all we may be told is the name of the father, the name of the child and the date of baptism. "20 August 1654. Ane chyld baptysed to Patrick Stewart called William" (Inverness, OPR98/1). Sometimes even the name of the child is omitted. Gradually it became more common to include the name of the mother, and it also became more usual to provide a designation for the father. Obviously the more detail, the more useful the record becomes for family researchers. The following entries are as informative as you have a right to expect.

19 November 1699 "Marjorie the Lawful daughter of James Peterkin gar[de]ner & Isabel Andersone in Tanachie was baptised. Witnesses:

Alexander Duncan in Moycarse & James Andersone." (Forres, OPR137/1)

12 July 1715 "Thomas son to James Brodie vintner in the Town and Grizel Moir his spouse was baptized. Witnesses: Thomas Boyd merchant in the Town and Thomas Moir." (Forres, OPR137/1)

"Robert lawful son of Andrew Stirling weaver Waterside and Christian Gilchrist his wife born 13th Jany 1802 bap 11th Feby." (Kirkintilloch, OPR498/3)

Witnesses were usually men but could be women. There were commonly two but could be more. Often their names are recognisable as members of the parents' families. They were perhaps the continuation of the Roman Catholic practice of having godparents. Indeed occasionally the words "godfather" and "godmother" are used instead of "witnesses". At some baptisms, instead of witnesses, one finds the phrase "in presence of the Congregation", suggesting that where witnesses were named the baptism may have taken place in the family home.

Baptism was an important event in Scottish family life which was often conducted at home, as reflected in this nineteenth century painting. (Aberdeen Art Gallery & Museums, John Phillip, 'Baptism in Scotland').

The name of the minister who carried out the ceremony may be included. This is in most cases the parish minister, but occasionally it can be the minister of "the Secession Church" or other dissenting church.

A clear distinction was made between legitimate and illegitimate children. A legitimate child would be described as "lawful" or its mother described as "spouse" of the father. An illegitimate child would be described as such or as "natural" or the entry might read "1716 October 23. Edward Dunbar in Coullodin had ane Child begot in furnecation with Isabel McGilchrist called Janet." (Inverness, OPR98/2)

Very occasionally, a minister may add a further relevant detail such as "The mother died immediately as the child was born" ; "The father being dead the child was presented by the mother"; "The child was presented by the grandfather William Couper because the father was out of the Country". (All from Stronsay in Orkney, OPR31/1)

Sometimes the baptisms of a whole family are recorded at once, regardless of dates of birth. Either this is the result of rather eccentric record-keeping or, more likely, the minister finding out that a family of children had not been baptised and encouraging the parents to remedy this unfortunate state. Not every child was baptised shortly after birth, particularly if that child had been born abroad and later was brought back to Scotland. In South Ronaldsay, "Alexander, son of Alexander Kennedy of Braehead, and his wife Agatha Isbister, born at Moose Lake, North America, 2nd February 1808, baptised here 26th May 1823." (OPR29/3)

Marriages

Until 1878, proclamation of banns in the parish church was an indispensable requisite of a regular marriage. The banns had to be proclaimed three times, on three successive Sundays. Occasionally all three times are recorded, more often only the date of the last proclamation is stated in the register. The date of the marriage might or might not be added: quite often there is a blank left for the date of marriage, not filled up. (This does not mean that the marriage did not take place.) Sometimes only the date of the marriage is given. Examples:

1716 June 15. "John Smart in Milden, and Isobel Drummie, daughter to John Drummie in Dalhasnie were contracted, and after being proclaimed several Lord's Dayes in ane orderly way, were married by the minister" on July 3. (Edzell, OPR285/2)

1797 September 29. "William Mackerras Lint Miller at Mills of Forres & Anna Grant daughter to John Grant at the Bridge End were contracted & after publication of the Banns were married 14th October." (Forres, OPR137/3)

1819 October 1. "There were booked in order to proclamation of marriage Hugh Milligan Labourer at Cardross and Anne Couper in Kilpatrick. They were married 25th October 1819 at Glasgow." (Old Kilpatrick, OPR501/3)

Note that "contracted" does not mean married, though in some instances it may mean that the banns have been proclaimed.

In these examples, the parties are fully described. In some cases, only their names may be given, presenting the researcher with the familiar problem of not knowing which Colin Campbell or Mary Macdonald that might be in a parish full of these names.

Marriage was a time of celebration, often involving the whole community.
(National Gallery of Scotland, David Allan, 'The Penny Wedding').

Sometimes the parties came from different parishes. That meant two separate proclamations of banns and entries in two parish registers. Thus in the parish of Kirkmichael in Perth-shire on 1823 June 14th "Peter Sim, in Righmore, parish of Caputh, and Anne Rattray in this parish" were contracted; and in the parish of Caputh that year "Peter Sim, at Easter Reimore in this parish, and Anne Rattray in the parish of Kirkmichael, having been proclaimed, were married July 1." (OPR370/3 and OPR337/5)

A few ministers provided additional information. A footnote to a marriage registered in Strontian in 1833 says "N.B. There has been something very odd about the above parties. They fast contracted & then split: then agreed, & with much regularity married. Were not married passing 5 days when lo. the weaker vessel set sail and steered her course for her mammy." (OPR505/2)

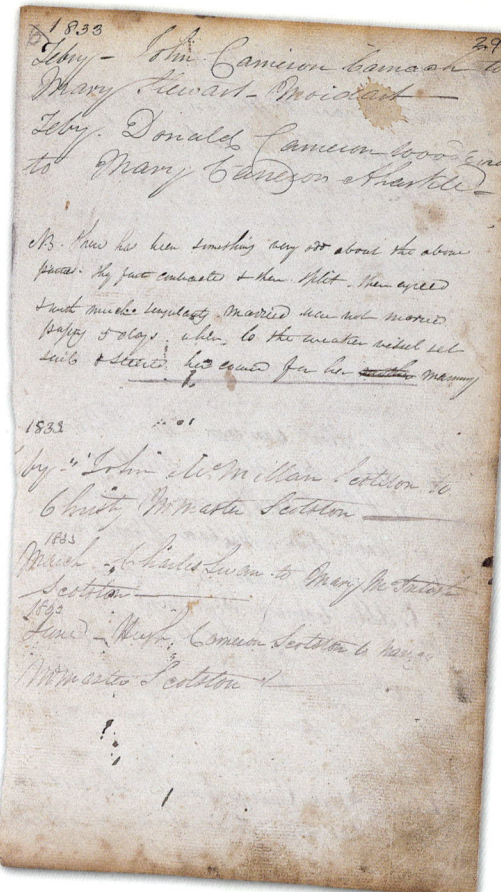

Second thoughts?
The footnotes recorded in the OPRs can reveal a lot more about events than just the names of people. This marriage entry for Strontian, Argyll-shire in 1833 shows that all was not well with the happy couple. "..the weaker vessel set sail and steered her course for her mammy". (OPR505/2)

Deaths and Burials

There are fewer records in this category than those of baptisms and marriages. You will find three distinct types of death/burial record, often within the same parish at different eras: mortcloth records; burial records; "bills of mortality".

Mortcloths have already been explained. The mortcloth records are the accounts for the loan of the parish mortcloth or mortcloths for burials within the parish. These were often contained within the kirk session accounts intermixed with such financial entries as the amount collected in the kirk on the Sabbath or payments to the poor of the parish, though sometimes mortcloth payments would be listed separately. Typical entries are: 1682 November 19 "received for ane Lend of the mortcloth to Robert Bryddies wife thirtie sh: Scots." (Falkland, OPR428/1)

16

1760 November 10 "The little plush Mortcloath to the corps of Archd McCasley son to Archd McCassley lying in Croft. 10d." (Abbey Parish, Renfrewshire, OPR559/5)

Burial records are simply a record of those who have been buried in the parish kirkyard. Again the information can be simply the name of the deceased or more full than that. Thus the register for Cruden tells us "1844 October 16. George Hutchison from the Gask, opposite the south grave of Alexander's tomb 1st length west stone." (OPR185/3) Probably the fullest entry ever occurs in the parish of Elie in 1787, where the record of the burial of Elizabeth Forrester, "relict of the deceased David Taylor in easter Town of Cultmalundy in the parish of Tippermuir, Perthshire and mother of Matthew Taylor Schoolmaster of Ely" is inordinately long. We learn the times of death and burial, the location of her grave, her state of health, about her parents, her birthplace, her children including a son who went to South Carolina and surmise about his fate, her sisters and her parents-in-law. Might it seem likely that the compiler of this register entry was her son, the schoolmaster? (OPR427/2)

Bills of mortality are simply annual lists of those who had died in the parish, giving the date of death, the name and usually the designation and sometimes

Eventually death comes to us all, and friends and neighbours would gather to pay their last respects. The sombre mood of the inevitable end to life is captured in this painting.
(Glasgow Museums & Art Galleries, James Guthrie, 'A Highland Funeral')

the age of the deceased. In coastal parishes, these may include the names of men who died at sea, as in the parish of Stronsay, "John Folsetter aged about 19 years was drowned on a herring-boat that was lost off Linksness on the 10th November 1818". (OPR31/1) In the same parish in 1837, when Betty Stevenson was found dead on the sea-shore: "strong suspicions were entertained by the community, that she had been murdered during the night." (OPR31/2)

Causes of death are rarely but occasionally given. In the parish of Loudoun in 1851, a whole series of children died of the measles, showing that there must have been an epidemic. (OPR603/4)

Though there was nothing to prevent kirk sessions continuing to compile their own records of baptisms etc, as official records the Old Parochial Registers stopped at the end of 1854. Population movements from rural parishes to the

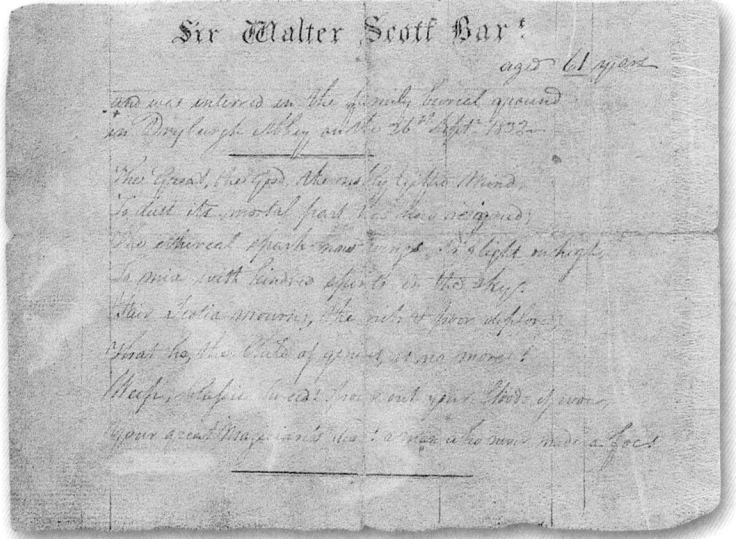

This 1832 death entry for Sir Walter Scott in the OPR for Melrose records where the writer died, where he was buried, and unusually his age at death.
It was felt that the passing of such an important author required a short composition:
"The Great, the Good, the nobly gifted mind.
To dust its mortal past has now resigned;
The ethereal spark now wings its flight on high,
To mix with kindred spirits in the sky.
Fair Scotia mourns, the rich and poor deplore,
That he the child of genius, is no more!
Weep, Classic Tweed! pour out your floods of woe,
Your great magician's dead! a man who never made a foe!   (OPR799/5)

towns had weakened parish control over the urban population at the same time as demands arose for a more accurate registration system. The Act which established the Registrar General's Department and compulsory registration instructed that all registers of births, deaths and marriages for every parish prior to 1st January 1855 were to be transmitted to this new department. All those made prior to 1820 were to be transmitted under the direction of the sheriff to the Registrar General for preservation in the General Register Office. Those dating from 1820 were to be delivered to the registrar of the parish. These were later also sent to the General Register Office. As few if any of the volumes conveniently ended at the close of 1819, these instructions presented problems. Volumes had to be split. If the records of births, marriages and deaths were intermixed with kirk session or other business, then copies had to be made for the interested party and the existing register brought to the Registrar General. "This copying must of necessity be an operation involving considerable difficulty, trouble and expense" wrote the first Registrar General in 1856.

But such manifold problems of splitting volumes, transcribing them and bringing in these valuable records to Edinburgh did proceed to the huge advantage of future researchers of family and social history. The latter may be further served by the occasional extra information to be found therein. The Dumfries register records the arrival of the Jacobite army there in 1745: "It is notable there was no sermon nor publick worship in the Churches of Dumfries on that memorable sabbath ... The young Pretender & the highland army were in possession of the town on Saturday, Sunday & Monday. Dumfries was full of tumult & confusion on the Lords day." (OPR821/2) In Deskford in 1740, a child was allegedly born with a wooden leg, presenting a conundrum to medical historians, who are unlikely to accept the contemporary suggestion that "the child has been got by a Chelsea pensioner with a timber hough". (OPR151/1) And if you want to find a 16th century cure for the common cold, you will find it in the register of baptisms for Aberdeen in 1588 (OPR168a/1): take garlic and hot milk and boil them together and drink it in the morning two or three days.

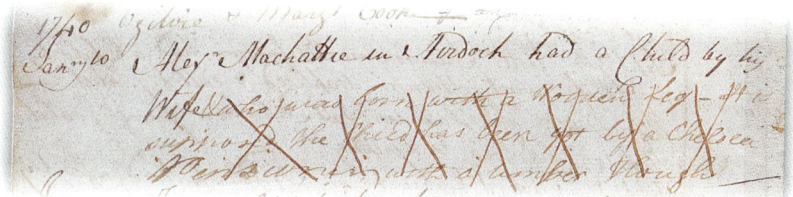

A medical miracle or local gossip? The scored text refers to a child born in Deskford, Banffshire in 1740, "who was born with a wooden leg". The father was alleged to be a Chelsea pensioner, a disabled ex-soldier with a wooden limb! (OPR151/1)

The Census Records

Because of a census, Christ was born in Bethlehem. This reminds us that the use of a census by governments as a means of gathering information about their subjects is of some antiquity. Long Before Christ, the Babylonians did it, as did the Egyptians and the Chinese. The information collected might be agricultural or commercial, but the most likely reasons were fiscal and military. The censuses of the Roman Empire were designed to discover who was liable to be taxed and how many men would be available for the Roman army.

Many censuses, at least in their preserved form, are simply an enumeration of the inhabitants for statistical purposes, not identifying individuals. Despite that, censuses have not always been popular, subject to a dislike of government prying or simple superstition about being counted. Indeed, when in the Old Testament King David enumerated his people, God Himself was so angry that He sent a pestilence upon the Israelites, which does seem odd of God and rather unfair. But this was remembered in Christian countries and in 1753 in the House of Commons, when a Bill to introduce a British census was defeated, the fear was expressed that a numbering of the people would be followed by "some great public misfortune or epidemical distemper".

Whatever the reason, census-taking fell out of favour for a long time after the fall of the Roman Empire and only got started again in the Western world in the 18th century. Enumerations of population took place in several European states from 1742 onwards. In the United States of America, a federal census began in

Census schedules were collected the day after the official census date. If you were out, then just leave it next door with a neighbour. (National Archives of Scotland: GRO6/380/3)

A snap-shot in time. The 1841 census was the first to enumerate entire households and family groups as shown by this example from Girthon in Kirkcudbrightshire. The ages given are not always accurate, as ages for those over 15 were rounded down to the nearest 5 years for ease of processing the statistics. (C.1841/866/5 page 2)

1790 to ensure an accurate distribution among the states of taxes and seats in the House of Representatives.

The earliest gathering of statistical information in Scotland was undertaken by the Rev Alexander Webster in 1755. He asked each parish minister to count the number of inhabitants in his parish, divided into Papists (Roman Catholics) and Protestants, and also to count the number of "fighting men", that is men between 18 and 56 years of age. It is interesting to note that in 1755 Glasgow had a population of 23,546, of whom none were Roman Catholic. Webster's "Census" is preserved in the National Library of Scotland and has been published.

In the United Kingdom, the Census was established in 1801 and has been carried out every ten years since (except 1941, because of wartime conditions). The 1801 Census was prompted by public concern about the growth of the population, and the economic and social effects this might have. From 1801 onwards, the questions asked in the Census are a guide to what the Government wanted to know: the size and age of the population, the houses they lived in, what work they did: a sort of national stocktaking.

From 1801 to 1831, in Scotland, the Censuses were carried out by the parish schoolmasters. They had to find out how many inhabited houses, houses being built and uninhabited houses there were in their parish; how many families were employed in agriculture, how many in trade, manufacture or handicrafts, and how many otherwise; and how many males and females. Whatever information had been gathered locally, only the summary figures were returned to a central point and made available to the public. However, thanks to the enthusiasm of a few schoolmasters, a very small number of lists of inhabitants were compiled and have survived locally (though not in the custody of the Registrar General). Thus, if you have ancestors in certain parishes in Orkney in 1821, you have a 20-year advantage over almost everyone else.

The Census of 1841 was the first to take the form of the Census as we recognise it today. Every person in the country on a specific night had to be named and described according to certain questions laid down by the Act of Parliament which authorised that Census. There were also questions about the houses in which people were living. In the 19th century, the Censuses were taken on the nights of 6/7 June 1841, 30/31 March 1851, 7/8 April 1861, 2/3 April 1871, 3/4 April 1881 and 5/6 April 1891.

Parishes and cities were divided into registration districts, containing up to about 200 houses. Each district was numbered and delineated in such terms as "So much of the Parish of Erskine as bounded by the river Clyde on the north, and the old Greenock High Road on the south, the parish of Inchinnan on the east, and the farms of East Longhaugh & West Porton on the west, including both these farms" (1841 Renfrewshire) or "Canongate Northside from 337 (head of Leith Wynd) to No 331 inclusive embracing Old Fleshmarket Close and Ramsay Court" (1871 Edinburgh).

Each district had an enumerator, who from 1861 was appointed by and answerable to the local registrar. In the week before the Census date, the enumerator had to deliver a schedule to each household in his district and to persuade the head of the household to complete the schedule by listing the inhabitants of that household and answering truthfully the questions asked about them. To refuse to answer or to answer a deliberate untruth was to render the householder liable to a penalty. The completed schedules were collected the day after the Census. The governor of any public or charitable institution (such as a prison, poorhouse or hospital) in which upwards of one hundred persons usually resided was appointed enumerator for that institution. The completed schedules were copied into the Census Enumeration Books for that district, which books were then sent to the central authority, who from 1861 was the Registrar General for Scotland. The information in these books was then used to compile such statistics as the Government required. The schedules were destroyed.

When you consult the Census records today, what you will read are the Census Enumeration Books from 1841 onwards. As the post of Registrar General for Scotland was not created until 1854, obviously he did not control the 1841 and 1851 Censuses. These were organised by the Home Office in

Large registration districts were divided into enumeration districts for the census. This plan of Perth shows the division of the city into its enumerated areas for the 1861 census. (GROS Collection)

22

London working with the assistance of the Scottish sheriffs and provosts. The Enumeration Books of 1841 and 1851 were removed to London, where they remained until 1910, when the Registrar General for Scotland found them "deposited in cellars in Westminster" and had them moved back to Edinburgh. The date is significant. Because of the Old Age Pensions Act of 1908, people over 70 needed to prove their age to obtain their pension, and for those whose baptism was omitted from the Old Parochial Registers, a Census might contain the necessary information. Thus from 1910, all the Scottish Census Enumeration Books from 1841 were together in the care of the Registrar General, though at that time not open to the general public.

Less information is provided by the 1841 Census than by its successors because fewer questions were asked. Within each place and house, what was sought was the name, surname, sex, age and occupation "of each person who abode in each house on the night of the 6th of June" and where each was born. Only one Christian name was allowed for each person. Common occupations were abbreviated, e.g. "M.S." for a male servant, "P.L.W." for power loom weaver. Birth places were vaguely expressed: "Yes" if born within the county, "No" if born elsewhere in Scotland, "E" if in England, "I" if in Ireland, "F" if a foreigner. Rather quirkily, for those over 15, the exact age was not given, ages being rounded down to the nearest 5 (i.e. those aged between 20 and 25 were all given as 20), presumably for statistical purposes.

Missing also from the 1841 Census, compared with later ones, are relationships. Families living together are listed together, so it possible to work out the likely family connection. Thus in Sugar House Lane in Greenock, Dugald McCallum, aged 40, ag[ricultural] lab[ourer], and Margaret McCallum, aged 30, with four McCallums aged below 7, the youngest unnamed at one month, are clearly one family. But in many households there are inhabitants with various names whose connection is not apparent. In the parish of Caputh at Riemore, Ann Sim aged 40 is presumably the mother of William Sim, a 15-year-old farmer, Peter Sim aged 13 and Margaret Sim aged 11, but who is David Gray aged 6? To find that out, one has to go to the OPR for the parish, which tells us that David is the illegitimate son of the Widow Sim (OPR337/5).

In the 1841 census, there was space for the schoolmaster of each parish to comment. This was usually just to confirm that boundaries were correct, but sometimes there are more valuable remarks, such as "The population of the parish of Carrington 1831 was 561 and the present census 1841 is 616, Increase 55, this influx arises from a Coal Work in the parish. None have emigrated from the parish for the Colonies or Foreign Countries, within the last 6 months". The 1851 Census contains similar helpful comments from the local ministers, such as "almost every Fisherman holds a small farm" (in the Shetland parish of Mid and South Yell).

The 1851 Census asked fuller basic questions which were repeated in subsequent Censuses. The head of each household had to supply for every person under their roof, their Christian names and surname; relation to head of family; "condition" (married, widowed or unmarried); age; rank, profession or occupation; where born; whether blind or deaf and dumb. Each Census expanded the questions asked. From 1861, the number of children of school age (5-15) and the number of rooms in the house with one or more windows were asked. From 1871 the householder was required to admit if anyone was imbecile, idiot or lunatic. The 1891 Census enquired who spoke Gaelic.

Clearly, the more information provided, the more valuable the record becomes to researchers, and the less guesswork required. Compare the 1841 entries with 1851 ones, such as the house in Church Lane in Lerwick, where the head was Christina Jameson, aged 35, a sailor's widow born in North Mavine, her household consisting of her three children, James a 12-year-old scholar born in Delting and Christina aged 8 and John aged 4 both born in Lerwick, but also of Barbara Matthewson, lodger, married, aged 45, a pauper, convict's wife, born in Unst: or the house at 104 Drysdale Street, Alloa, which contained not only the householder James Melvin, house carpenter, his wife and children but also two older un-married brothers, John Melvin, an architect and housebuilder employing six men, and Archibald Melvin, a house carpenter, employing three men.

This Edinburgh census entry for 1861 shows the family of the infant Arthur Conan Doyle, then aged one. The family lived at Picardy Place in the city centre, and the entry reveals that his mother came from Ireland. (C.1861/685.2/90)

24

In the Old Parochial Registers, married women retained their maiden surname in the Scottish fashion. The Censuses were ruled by English customs and therefore married women appear under their husband's surname. There was also a Victorian tendency to alter some Christian names which were deemed not quite proper, so that many ladies called Jane in the Census were actually named Jean and some called Janet were better known as Jessie. For example, Jessie McDonald or Hutchinson (1805-1882), who lived in Braemar, was called Jess or Jessie at her marriage and the baptisms of her children, in the 1841-61 censuses, on her death certificate and on her gravestone, but is called Janet in the 1871 and 1881 censuses.

Where persons were not actually related to the head of the family, their "relation" might be servant, lodger or visitor.

The age column in the schedule was divided into males and females, whose ages were totalled separately for statistical purposes.

The rank, profession or occupation information is of particular interest, showing which occupations were prevalent in which areas, which were increasing and which decreasing. The Census reports will tell you how many innkeepers there were in Dunbartonshire, how many coal miners in Lanarkshire, how many milliners in Dumfriesshire, and so on. Many 19th century jobs now seem quaint to us: artificial feather maker, book folder, cane chair worker, cork cutter, envelope maker, marker in a billiard room (a 12-year-old boy), scavenger, stocking knitter, tobacco spinner, venetian blind painter, washerwoman.

In the countryside, farmers and agricultural labourers still loomed large. The acreage farmed and the labourers employed by a farmer were usually expressed, such as "farmer 1300 acres employing 14 labourers". Obtaining this information occasionally troubled the enumerators. A farmer might occupy land in more than one county, in which instance his acreage and servants might be partially assigned to the wrong locality. Also, were members of a farmer's family to be included in the number of labourers employed? It was decided that wives and daughters who acted as dairymaids in addition to their ordinary domestic duties were not to be included, but sons and daughters employed as outdoor labourers were to be so.

Not everyone of course had a recognised occupation. Wives and daughters often had a blank in this column. But under "Rank, Profession or Occupation" you may find gentlewoman, annuitant, pauper, crofter's sister, tenant's niece, farmer's mother, farmer's aged and infirm widow. Some of these descriptions do suggest that woman's work was an occupation.

If a person was born in Scotland, the parish of birth was to be stated; if in England, Wales or Ireland, the county; if abroad, the country. These birthplaces showed how mobile society was becoming. Admittedly, particularly in rural areas, many people lived their lives in the parish in which they were born. For example, in 1871 the Matheson family at Tarsveg in the parish of Sleat, five brothers and two sisters, all unmarried aged 19 to 35 had all been born in that parish. But other families travelled widely, wherever work took them. Thus, in 1861, at Glenbuck in the parish of Muirkirk, John Short, age 25, a coal miner, had been born in Ireland, while his wife and three infant sons had each been born in different parishes in Lanarkshire and Ayrshire; and in Carrubers Close in Edinburgh, James Muirhead, age 31, horse dealer's man, had been born in Rutherglen, his wife had been born in Newburn in Fife and his children in Edinburgh, Liverpool and Glasgow. The origins of the members of one household might be diverse. At 6 Crawfurd Road in Edinburgh in 1891, Edward Muriset, the head, a teacher of French, had been born in Switzerland; his wife Marian, headmistress of a private school, came from Ireland; their young son Oliver was born in Edinburgh; their boarder, James Copland, assistant curator, Historical Department, General Register House, had been born in Kirkwall in Orkney; while the servant, Dolina MacLeod came from Duirinish in Skye.

In some parishes, one may note the influx of railway labourers from Ireland. Indeed, the population of a parish could be temporarily doubled by the presence of navvies and other railway workers. In his 1871 report, the then Registrar General was hardly politically correct when he commented "it is painful to contemplate what may be the ultimate effect of this Irish immigration on the morals and habits of the people, and on the future prospects of the Country."

In the 1891 Census, the householder's schedule required everyone to say whether they spoke Gaelic only or both Gaelic and English. There had been a trial run of this subject in 1881, when there was no such question in the schedule, but the enumerators were instructed to discover who spoke Gaelic. This showed that the language was prevalent in the northern and western Highlands. In 1881, 75% of the population of Sutherland had the Gaelic, but the 1891 enquiry showed that most Gaelic speakers also spoke English, apart from those in a few parishes in the Western Isles. One can also note class and generation distinctions arising. A typical example in 1891 is in the parish of Golspie, where at Kirkton House (27 windowed rooms) Alexa Murray, age 61, a widow and farmer, and her two servants spoke both Gaelic and English,

Top: The 1891 census was the first to formally introduce a question on Gaelic-speaking. This example from St Kilda shows that in isolated communities few people could speak English. (C.1891/111.4);
Bottom: Group of St Kildans, taken at the turn of the 20th century. (Scottish Life Archive)

while her three grown daughters did not speak Gaelic. Some registrars were uncertain whether occasional use of Gaelic counted. They were told "the Registrar-General thinks the expression in question may properly be held to apply to all persons who are so familiar with the Gaelic as to be able to converse fluently in that language". Only Scottish Gaelic counted. Irish Gaelic speakers entered in schedules in Dumbarton had to be removed from the Enumeration Books.

One house might contain several families, which were distinguished by a mark between them in the enumeration books. Making the distinction sometimes was not easy. Many householders let out rooms to other families or to individual lodgers. Were these tenants all part of one household or did they form separate households? It was decided that those who received board as well as bed formed part of the same household, but lodgers who found their own meals formed separate households. The same applied to servants. Farm servants who slept in outhouses were to be included in their master's schedule, if the master fed them. A public institution (e.g. hospital, barracks, a rescue home for fallen women) was treated as one household. But inns, hotels, lodging houses were not public institutions, and in them there could be several heads of households. In 1861, the registrar for Carluke was concerned "whether a person travelling from place to place, and who may occupy part of a bed for perhaps only one night is ... to be regarded as a separate occupier." In 1891, the registrar for Arrochar "ranked some dozen Navvies huts containing each some 30 beds as houses not considering each lodger as a family which in this case would be misleading. We must just hold the keeper of the hut responsible for the number of inmates most of them are illiterate and they cannot be altogether trusted for filling the schedule correctly."

Defining what constituted a house also caused difficulties. The Scottish system of flats as separate feudal properties meant that Scottish houses did not all have an entrance from the street. Subdivided flats added to the problem. The 1881 Census finally defined a house in Scotland as "(1) every dwelling with distinct outside entrance from a street, court, lane, road, etc, or (2) with a door opening directly into a common stair, but any such dwelling, if subdivided and occupied by different families, is reckoned as only a single house."

Houses had to be dwelling houses. Buildings such a churches and warehouses and others not intended as dwelling houses were ignored in most Censuses. However, in 1851 and only in 1851, it was decided to collect statistics of the accommodation afforded by various Churches and other places of Public Worship and of the number of people attending public worship on Sunday March 30th: also of the existing educational establishments and the number of scholars under instruction. Enumerators had to issue different schedules to churches and schools (not the householder's one). These returns show the diversity of churches, mostly Protestant, and the variety of types of schools, the great majority parish schools or supported by the Church of Scotland or the Free Church. Sabbath and evening schools were counted, as were literary and scientific institutions in each parish, such as in the county of Clackmannan the Alloa Phrenological Society and the Tillicoultry Mechanics Library. There were many subscription libraries in Scotland.

On a Census night, not all persons might be sleeping in a building. Therefore at the end of each enumerator's book were entered those who had slept in barns, sheds, caravans, tents etc., in mines or pits or in the open air. The police were directed to assist the enumerators in tracing any such. Thus in 1861 in the parish of Newlands, Thomas Chisholm, age 40, a farmer of 135 acres, was "Out of doors with sheep" at a fair; and in the parish of Muirkirk a family was "found in a travelling caravan, containing wild animals". These travellers were no exotic foreigners but a Scottish family, headed by William Turnbull, showman, born in St Ninians, his wife born in Alloa, his unmarried brother and three children, born in St Ninians, Musselburgh and England.

Census returns record the whereabouts of itinerant or migrant populations of workers who were involved in seasonal work, particularly on the land. Many people may not have been located in their usual place of residence on census night. (Scottish Life Archive).

Those who were aboard vessels had also to be counted. Vessels in rivers or inland waters were the responsibility of the enumerators. But vessels in ports were attended by the customs officers. Before the Census date, the Registrar General wrote to the foreign consuls at the ports, requesting their assistance, as the crews and passengers of all vessels had to take part, not just British ones. In 1891 the Norwegian vice-consul at Peterhead had a sad problem when all but one of the crew of a Norwegian vessel perished on the coast of Crimond on the night of the Census. The survivor appears in the return for the parish of Crimond where he passed the remainder of the night after his rescue.

The question about the number of rooms with windows obviously showed the relative prosperity within a parish and of individual families. In the parish of Sleat in 1871, most households were lucky to have two windows, but the house at Isleornsay of Daniel Fraser, a general merchant employing two men, had no less than fourteen windows. Daniel was doing well. His household also included a governess to educate his children. In the poorer areas of the cities, many households had only one window.

In studying the Census records, we have to remember that what they show is a snapshot at a particular point in time. The same questions asked a day or a week

29

or a month or a year later would produce different answers. On the chosen day (a Sunday), the majority of people would be in their own homes, but some would not. Those whose professions took them away from home, such as fishermen or commercial travellers, might be recorded in quite another parish from their own. Some people now went on holiday, say to Cumbrae for the sea bathing. People might be visiting relatives. In 1841 in Newton Stewart in the parish of Penninghame, we find a household consisting of Margaret Gordon, age 30, and three young children. But we happen to know that Margaret had a husband and two other young children and therefore we have to search further in that parish Census. The husband was not in the parish that day, but one child was in the household of James Vernon, age 55, shoemaker, and the other in the household of James Vernon, age 31, also shoemaker, whom we believe to be their maternal grandfather and uncle. What we do not know is whether these children were just spending the night with their relatives or were farmed out to them for an extended period. The Censuses provide many answers but sometimes offer us new unanswered questions.

Like any of man's creations, the Censuses are liable to human error. The head of a household might, deliberately or accidentally, provide inaccurate information. An inattentive enumerator might make a slip in copying a schedule into his book. The vast majority of the details in the Censuses are likely to be accurate, but no human endeavour will be one hundred per cent perfect.

Despite the threat of punishment, some people lied, whether out of vanity or perhaps disguising their origins. In Ballachulish in 1871, an "educated lady" was caught out when she insisted that her age was 29, when the parochial register of baptisms showed that she was 44. Looking from one Census to the next, people do not always age by ten years, though in some cases the head of the household may have passed on such information in good faith, and some people may have genuinely not been certain of their year of birth.

Where there are errors or apparent errors, most were probably not intentional. In the parish of Crathie and Braemar in 1841, 6-year-old George Hutchinson appears twice, once in his father's house in Castletown of Braemar along with his siblings, and also, described (humorously?) as an agricultural labourer, in the household of his maternal grandfather in Inverey, where he was presumably visiting. Doubtless both his father and grandfather completed their respective schedules genuinely The problem of course is that an error may only be recognised when compared with information from other sources.

The Census staff had other problems. Those employed on the Census, supported by the Registrar General, complained consistently that they received inadequate remuneration. While the registrars had some discretion in the sizes of the enumerator's districts, the division into districts could involve a lot of work, especially in Glasgow with its ever increasing population and extending boundaries. In 1891 the Boundary Commissioners were readjusting boundaries of counties and parishes at the same time as the Census was underway. A parish boundary might run through a farm. One registrar might accuse another of poaching a house from his district. In 1881 an enumerator in Stenscholl refused to go into houses where there was an outbreak of fever, and one in Kilmacolm was refused admission by a recluse, so completed the schedule himself. Some high-ranking householders could also be difficult, such as the Earl of Glasgow who in 1861 refused to say the number of windowed rooms in Hawkhead House in Paisley (perhaps he feared a return of the window tax?). After the Census had been taken in Glasgow in 1871, some enumerator's books had to be rewritten. Those for the district of Glenelg in 1891 were lost, and then found. "The drawer in which the Books had been kept had no back, and they had fallen down behind the drawers." Returns from distant and inaccessible districts such as St Kilda arrived very late. All these problems and many others assailed the busy Registrar General.

Once the enumerator's books had been brought into Edinburgh, there was more work to be done in the Registrar General's department. Two permanent officers were appointed to act as superintendents, regulating a team of temporary clerks (26 in number in 1881 and 1891) supplied by the Civil Service Commissioners. These clerks had to be aged between 16 and 40 and had been examined in arithmetic, orthography, handwriting and intelligence. Their task was to draw out from the Census records the statistical information which the Government required. They of course did not have the benefit of computers but in 1891 the Registrar General was permitted to purchase a new arithmometer or calculating machine to assist their work.

As a result of this work, after each Census there was issued (since 1861 by the Registrar General) a voluminous report containing analysis and statistical tables. These reports were presented to both Houses of Parliament in London and were available to the public. The numerous tables calculated by nation, county, parish and burgh every possible comparative viewpoint of population, age, occupation, birthplace, houses, etc. The information provided to the government of the state of the housing, health, education and occupations of the population was clearly of immense value. The Scotsman

Census records hold a wealth of detail about family life and household composition. Families were much larger than today, as shown in this photograph of the Law family of Craighill, St Cyrus, Kincardineshire, c.1900. (Scottish Life Archive)

newspaper wrote that the 1871 report "of the facts collected at the late Census of Scotland is worth its weight in gold to the statist, the historian, and the students of all social and sanitary matters".

While the statistics were freely available, the information provided by householders in their schedules and repeated in the enumerator's books were regarded as strictly confidential. Successive governments up to the present day were and are convinced that people would not answer the Census questions if they thought anyone other than a few government officials, sworn to secrecy, would read their answers. The Registrar General regularly assured the public "The facts will be published in General Abstracts only, and strict care will be taken that the returns are not used for the gratification of curiosity." The public were assured that no information about named individuals would be passed by the Census Office to any other Government department or any other authority or person. If anyone employed in taking the Census disclosed information improperly, he was liable to prosecution.

Of course, enquiries were received from both official bodies and private individuals seeking access to information locked within the census returns. Most were refused though the Registrar General did have a discretion. School boards which wanted to find out the identities of children of school age in their district were not given that information. The Crown Agent was declined access when he was investigating a criminal case. But the Medical Officer for Glasgow was allowed access, because it was considered that the enormous size and population of that city would make people less suspicious of their details being improperly used. As already said, after 1908, individuals were provided with age information to prove their entitlement to an old age pension. But in 1911 a man who needed to prove his age to obtain a particular job was refused, being told that if the Census returns were "to be available to prove the age of anyone who chose to ask to have the Returns consulted, the work of the Department would be very largely increased and the Census would be used for purposes for which it was never intended." Yet a kindly Registrar General did check the age of a lady approaching 100 years, and in 1922 the Registrar General proposed that the returns for 1841 to 1871 be opened to the public. The Scottish Office was not keen but in 1923 was finally persuaded to allow this. However, any searches had to be done by the Registrar General's staff. Members of the public were not allowed direct access, except for officers of local authorities or "other specially approved applicants".

The question of public access remained a difficult issue. As the 20th century progressed, demands for freedom of information and a huge growth in interest in the genealogical content of the Census records faced increasing concerns about confidentiality in relation to people still alive. Access became both easier and more restricted. The 1923 situation remained unaltered until 1955, when the returns for 1881 and 1891 were opened and the public was allowed direct access to the Census records up to 1891 in New Register House. Eventually in 1974 government ministers decided that in future Scottish Census returns would not be made available until 100 years after the Census to which they relate. This decision brought Scotland into line with English practice, on the principle that, in a matter of such public importance, policy should be uniform throughout the United Kingdom. Thus in the year 2000 we can "gratify our curiosity" up to the year 1891. The 1901 Census returns will be made available to the public in January 2002.

The Statutory Registers of Births, Deaths and Marriages

The Old Parochial Registers served the people of Scotland for three hundred years, not always consistently, as we have seen. While the 19th century saw an overall improvement in the keeping of these registers through much of the country, it also saw an increasing failure to record all the events which they were supposed to record. In brief, after 1800, the industrialisation of Scotland proceeded apace, and with that huge migrations of the population from rural parishes to the larger burghs. In particular, the cities became urban conurbations, with the poorer classes crammed into insanitary tenements. In the countryside, the parish system still worked, but in the slums of the cities the ministers and the session clerks lost control of and often did not know their parishioners.

At the same time there was a growing interest in medical science, in social reform and in statistics as a means of understanding and controlling social change. Health professionals and reformers were keen to know what diseases affected the population, at what age different classes or occupations of people died, and how conditions could be improved. The Censuses demonstrated the size and age of the population. Statisticians proved that far more people were born and died in the country than were recorded in the Old Parochial Registers.

Arguments grew for the introduction of a system of compulsory registration of births, deaths and marriages, operated centrally by the Government. In this respect, Scotland lagged behind the rest of Western Europe, which mostly accepted the system introduced by the Emperor Napoleon I in France. Among the legal reforms enacted by the Napoleonic Code in 1804 was the removal of responsibility for registration from the Church to the State. Exact provisions were specified for informants, registrars and register books and what the entries in the books should contain. This system was introduced into Belgium, Switzerland and some states in what is now Germany.

Following a report of a Select Committee of the House of Commons, compulsory registration was introduced into England in 1837. The Act establishing this divided England into registration districts each with a registrar, who were supervised by superintendent registrars. The registrars had to record all births, deaths and marriages occurring in their districts, and those involved were compelled to inform the registrar of all relevant details, which included the cause of death. Copies of the registers were transmitted to the General Register Office in London.

Scotland had to wait another 18 years to follow suit. In the 1830s, several attempts were made to introduce a Bill in the House of Commons, but fell because they charged the parties registering with payment of fees. In the succeeding years, reports and petitions in favour of registration came from concerned bodies such as the British Association, the Royal Colleges of Physicians and Surgeons in Edinburgh and the Life Assurance Offices of Scotland.

In 1847, the Lord Advocate, Lord Rutherfurd, introduced a Bill for registration in Scotland. In the next two years, this Bill twice passed the House of Lords, but twice got stuck in the House of Commons.

Civil registration of births, deaths and marriages was introduced in Scotland from 1 January 1855. Posters were printed in both English & Gaelic to enable everyone to understand their responsibilities under the new law. It was compulsory to register but free of charge, and was therefore an immediate success. (GROS Collection)

There were three problems. The Bill was unwisely tied to an unpopular measure to reform the Scottish law of marriage; schoolmasters were disqualified from being registrars; and it involved expense to the Government. The medical and insurance professions might be in favour, but the Church of Scotland was opposed.

The General Assembly objected to the Bill in its current form. There were also petitions against the Bill from individual presbyteries and kirk sessions and from schoolmasters and session clerks. Naturally, the Church was loath to lose control to the State of this influential function, but the main concern was the loss of status and income to the session clerks who were usually schoolmasters. In 1852, the General Assembly set up a committee to consider the registration of births, marriages and deaths. This committee admitted that the existing registers were inadequate and proposed that a compulsory system under the central control of a superintending board should be established by legislation. But this system should retain the existing machinery, so that the session clerks be not deprived.

In 1854 was at last achieved "An Act to provide for the better Registration of Births, Deaths and Marriages in Scotland". This Act sought to establish and maintain a complete and uniform system of registration in Scotland of all births, deaths and marriages from the 1st of January 1855. The Government would provide an office for "The General Registry Office of Births, Deaths and Marriages" in which the registers were to be preserved, and would appoint a Registrar General of Births, Deaths and Marriages in Scotland. Existing session clerks would be the local registrars, but thereafter these registrars were to be appointed by the parochial boards or, in the burghs, by the town councils. Registers were to be kept in duplicate, one copy to be kept by the local registrar and one copy sent to the custody of the Registrar General.

The Act attempted "to combine the utmost degree of efficiency with the utmost degree of economy". Money was to be saved by housing the Registrar General in the existing General Register House (built to house the department now known as the National Archives of Scotland) and by not having superintendent registrars. Their role was to be filled by the sheriffs, who were to receive no extra remuneration, being paid well enough as it was. However, within a year, it was deemed necessary to create the post of examiners to inspect the registers and they had to be paid. And by 1861 it had become necessary to provide a separate building for the "Registry Office" in Edinburgh, which is the custom-built New Register House where the registers are stored and where the public may now consult them.

Registration was compulsory and free. Local registrars were paid so much per entry in their registers, but that sum was met by local assessment. The Treasury met the central expenses of the Registrar General. However, there were financial penalties for late registration. Anyone guilty of false registration could be punished by imprisonment or transportation to penal settlements in the colonies. Annual indexes were compiled for each register and fees were charged for consulting them, as there were for consulting a register and for obtaining an extract (except for the first extract supplied freely to the informant of the event).

The country was divided into registration districts, usually existing parishes. Each district had its own registrar. In the cities, there might be enough work for a full-time registrar, but in most of the country the local registrars were inevitably part-time. The parish councils liked to appoint those who were already public servants, both because their qualities were known and to enable them to eke out their small salaries. The majority were schoolmasters or inspectors of the poor, but any suitable man who lived in and knew the locality might be appointed. They could be a shopkeeper, postmaster, farmer, joiner, etc.

Registrars were rarely provided with accommodation and had to set up their office in their own house or working premises. This could make for inconvenience. The registrar might live or work some way from a main road. In 1855, the parishioners of Chapel of Garioch complained about the office of the registrar (the school) being at one side of a large parish and when people reached there "they are subjected to the very disagreeable necessity of disclosing the object of their visit in the hearing of his scholars in ... the schoolroom where they are taught." No chance of the neighbours not knowing their business.

Every registrar could appoint an assistant registrar, to act in case of his illness or unavoidable absence. Naturally, many appointed their sons, though others such as the local minister might be selected. Women, such as daughters, were specifically barred from this job, though some seem to have been employed, whether officially or not. Of the registrar of Pitsligo in 1876, an examiner commented "His sister is said to have done much of ... the work, as I suspect many other sisters & daughters & wives do!"

The examiners' reports are a fine source of information about the registrars and their competence. The great majority were hard-working, careful men, but there were exceptions, particularly in the early days. Old age was not necessarily a handicap. The registrar of Clyne in 1899 "who is 80 years of age did very good work", but a more typical comment was of the Blairgowrie registrar in 1856 "a palsied old man". In 1900 an examiner complained that "There is a tendency on the eastern District to give Registrarships to men too old to learn the work." He pointed out to the town clerk of Arbroath "that persons incapable of doing other business should not be appointed compassionately to the office of Registrar."

There were other problems. A registrar might appear to be incompetent or insufficiently interested in the work. The registrar of Forgan in 1856 was a young man "evidently more in love with himself than with any part of his business". The Aberlour man in 1865 spent too much of his time "fiddling and fishing". Registrars could fall ill, die suddenly or even abscond. In 1874 the registrar of Glenmuick vanished along with the duplicate register for 1873. And there was the inevitable occurrence of intemperance. Fortunately for himself, the registrar of Weem in 1860 turned teetotal when he married. Getting rid of a registrar was not easy. He could only be removed by the sheriff on the petition of the parochial board or burgh magistrates or the Registrar General. Mr Alexander Dewar, the registrar for the Milton district in Glasgow, was accused in 1900 of being in a regular state of intoxication at work, but the sheriff merely warned him. Perhaps Mr Dewar was only carrying on tradition: in 1855 it was said that the registrar of Milton had been in a state of perpetual intoxication for two months.

As the entries in the registers were handwritten, all registrars were expected to write neatly and legibly. We can judge for ourselves if they always did! Some were criticised by the examiners, with such complaints as "the handwriting here is not of the bold & plain sort that is so desirable in these records. It is effeminate in its style" (Inchture, 1856) and "Penmanship execrable & spelling bad" (Prestonpans, 1876). There were also complaints about the quality of the ink. Poor ink might fade. Registrars were supposed to use good ink from recommended suppliers and no blotting paper. There were to be no erasures in the registers, even of blots. Mistakes made before any entries were signed had to be scored through but left legible.

To keep the registers safe, the registrars were originally instructed to have a strong iron box, but from 1860, the sheriff could direct the parochial board or town council to provide a fire-proof safe. This advisable precaution was not always followed. In 1875 a fire in the manse of Glenrinnes consumed the previous year's books not yet transmitted to the Registrar General.

Birth entry for the architect and designer Charles Rennie Mackintosh, born in 1868, which includes his father's signature. For the first time a uniform record could now be maintained about such 'vital events'. The format of the registers and the information recorded remained virtually unchanged until the mid-1960s. (B.1868/644.1/1360)

Registrars did not just wait until they were voluntarily notified by the families concerned of births, deaths and marriages. They were required to keep themselves informed of any such events happening in their district, to ensure that all were registered, by close contact with those such as ministers, midwives and undertakers.

Once a year in almost all registration districts, an examiner would arrive to inspect the books. Foula and Fair Isle were inspected only every fifth year and St Kilda every tenth year. The examiners did a lot of travelling, covering huge areas, as much as nine counties. In 1860, one examiner wrote "During the past season I have examined the Register Books, and relative documents, of 242 parishes or districts - have travelled about 2780 miles, and have been officially employed, and from home, for 230 days." Their reports make for fascinating reading. They commented not only on the character and competence of the registrars, but also on individual entries of births, deaths and marriages, and on larger social matters which impressed them.

Their comments on the individual entries in the registers were sometimes in the nature of a clarification, particularly where there were variations in surnames. Registrars were supposed to accept the spelling they were given, whatever their or the examiners' doubts. Members of the same family could spell their surname "Dods" or "Dodds", "Neelson", "Nelson" or "Neilson". In Tarbert in 1876, a son had adopted the spelling of "Maclaine" while his parents were always known as "Maclean". Some people, legitimately born, caused perplexity by having adopted their mother's or stepfather's surname. Discrepancies between signatures and entered names occurred. Registrars were advised not to put too much trust in signatures: "a ploughman may sign one way today and another tomorrow." But the registrar at Knockbaan in 1858 was probably wrong in entering the father of a baby as "Harold" when he signed "Torquil" which the registrar believed to be the Gaelic for Harold.

It was not just Gaelic names which troubled the officials. Parents had total freedom to choose the Christian names of their child, but sometimes a registrar or examiner might consider a name unsuitable. Eventually, in the future interests of the child, registrars were advised by the Registrar General to try to discourage parents from giving their children abbreviated names such as "Tom", "Alex" or "Minnie" or fanciful names such as "May Peace Reign" (in 1920). Parents were also pressurised not to give a recognised male name to a female child (or vice versa) or to give the same name to two children in the one family. But stubborn parents could insist and ignore the registrar's wise advice.

Other comments by the examiners add to the information supplied in the registers, and where these comments refer exactly to a specific entry they may further satisfy the ancestor researcher. In 1865, there occurred in Tradeston, Glasgow, the death of a man who "had been connected with Dr Livingstone's expedition in the capacity of Engineer". In 1892 in Gladsmuir, died a woman "who was the last survivor of the old coal carriers employed at Penston Coal pits. The Act abolishing female employment in mines was passed in 1843." Some remarks were more frivolous: "The bridegroom ... was drowned in the Dee during last winter. It is feared too much Lochnagar had to do with it" (Crathie, 1876). Some indeed could supply the basis for a work of fiction. The death took place in West Calder in 1865 of "Andrew Waugh a landed Proprietor. His father was a labourer. He (Andrew) fortunately hurt himself in a quarry when at work and took a small shop. He throve, and died a laird." And there was an unfortunate marriage in Carriden the same year "The lady was in the Perth Penitentiary when the banns were complained. A thief. She blessed her husband by leaving him 2 or 3 days after marriage, and is said to be now a Strumpet in Glasgow."

Perhaps more significant were the general social observations, such as the lack of undertakers in country districts; drunkenness at rural marriages; the way whole families in northern coastal parishes migrated during the fishing season; the high proportion of illegitimate children among the poorer classes who died in infancy; the exceptionally high mortality in the aftermath of an influenza epidemic; the dividing of school holidays to allow for "potato lifting" in October. That last inconvenienced an examiner in 1900; as did the lack of an inn in Pencaitland in 1860, which was attributed to the presence of a teetotaller of substance in the parish. In 1910 in Lanarkshire, the large number of Polish miners with little knowledge of English made difficulties for the registrars.

The 1854 Act specified what particulars had to be registered. Fuller details were recorded than in England, making the Scottish registers of particular value for family researchers. For the year 1855, even more information was recorded in the birth, death and marriage registers than thereafter. It was then realised that too much was being asked of the registrars and an Amending Act reduced the amount of detail they had to investigate. In the birth registers for 1855 and them only, you will find the ages and birthplaces of the father and mother, and the number of other children of the parents, whether living or deceased. In the death registers for 1855 and them only, you will find the place of birth of the deceased, how long he or she had been in the district where the death occurred, the names and ages of any children living or deceased, and the place of burial and name of the undertaker. In the marriage registers for 1855 and them only, you will find the birthplaces of the parties and the number of any children by former marriages, living or dead.

From 1856, the particulars to be entered in the register of births were as follows.

(1) The surname and Christian names of the child. An illegitimate child would usually have its mother's surname (which might be her married name). It could only have its father's surname if both father and mother requested it and both father and mother signed the register as informants of the birth. If a child was legitimated by the subsequent marriage of its parents, then that fact was noted in the margin of the birth entry. If a child's Christian names had not been chosen at the time of registration or were changed shortly afterwards, perhaps at its baptism, these names could be inserted in the register in the period of six months after registration. Longer than that required the sheriff's written authority. Some short-lived children might have no names at all. In the Canongate in 1865 died a child only known as "The Bangholm foundling".

(2) Year, day of the month and hour when the child was born, and the name of the place, including the street and house number. Of course not all children were born in buildings. One may find locations such as a caravan on Glasgow Green. Quite a few children have been born in an ambulance. Indeed with some children the place and time of birth might not be known. When a child was found exposed and the mother could not be traced, then the date and time and place recorded were those of when and where it had been found. The precise time of birth was important in the case of twins.

(3) The child's sex, male or female. This was not always obvious! In cases of doubt, the registrar might require the parents to produce the child to him.

(4) The father's names, surname, rank, profession or occupation, the names and maiden and former married surnames of the mother, and (except between 1856 and 1860) the date and place of marriage. The information of the mother's names and the marriage is invaluable to family researchers. Parties might have to produce proof of the date and place of their marriage.

(5) The signature, designation and residence of the informant. Qualified informants were one of the parents or, in the event of death, illness or inability, the person in charge of the child or the occupier of the house where the child was born or the nurse present at the birth. If the informant was present

at the birth, then the word "Present" was added. However, as the Regulations for Registrars reasonably pointed out "Where the mother happens to be the informant, the insertion of the word (Present) is, of course, unnecessary."

(6) The date when the entry was made, and the signature of the Registrar.

Still-born children were not recorded in either the birth or death registers, though children who breathed only for moments had to be entered in both. Since 1939, there has been a separate register of still-births, but it is closed to public searchers.

The number of illegitimate births was a cause for concern. An examiner commented in 1860, "Illegitimacy is too common. It is not unusual for mothers to request their daughters may sign the entry at a different time from the fathers of their illegitimate children, their object being to prevent the parties meeting. The effect of such meeting has given rise to resumption of elicit [sic] intercourse." Many illegitimate children were of course a product of stable relationships, perhaps where the woman had started a new partnership after being deserted by her husband (who might have gone to America).

A positive consequence of illegitimacy was adoption. Adoption was not legally recognised in Scotland until 1930, but obviously it had always occurred. While the great majority of informal adoptions were not recorded, where the matter was drawn to their attention, registrars might record an adoption. For example, the registrar of Bo'ness was allowed to add to his register of births "The child whose birth is recorded in Ent. No 166 in the Regr Book of Births for the year 1872 has - with the consent of its mother - been adopted by Thos Grant, engine keeper, and his wife; and the child will henceforth bear the names Thomina Georgina Hunter Grant." However, the child's original surname remained unaltered at her birth registration entry. From 1930, the Registrar General has kept a register of adopted children, which is open to the general public, though the link between a birth entry and an adoption entry is kept strictly confidential.

It was not only the birth of illegitimate children which troubled examiners and others, but also their frequently early death. While this may in some cases have been caused by the poverty and inadequacy of the mother, more sinister causes were suspected. In particular, the examiner of the Dundee area in 1855 noted the number of infants who died shortly after birth, with no proper medical attendance. "The informants in those cases are commonly elderly women of the most suspicious appearance & character ... who can scarcely tell their errand to the Registrar, without betraying a guilty blush." The alleged cause of death was often "bowel hive, which respected medical practitioners consider neither more nor less, than a convenient term for accidentally overlaying or smothering a child." The examiner further remarked "the victims are almost universally children of the lowest and most intemperate class of society." There was a notable lack of sympathy for those subjected to extreme poverty. However, in subsequent years, perhaps as a result of the publicity given to the examiner's views, deaths from "bowel hive" were much reduced. But the problem did not disappear. In 1866, the examiner for the South of Scotland, noting such early deaths, suspected that unwanted children were being exposed to the severity of the weather or refused sufficient food.

Illegitimacy was for life. When the illegitimate person died, the word "illegitimate" was, until 1919, recorded on their death registration entry. Many respectable married persons, dying in the fullness of their years, carried this stigma to their graves.

Some causes of death were less than natural. The entry in the register of deaths of George Bryce in 1864 records that he was hanged by the public executioner at the head of Liberton Brae in Edinburgh for the murder of Jane Seton. The register does not reveal that Bryce was left to struggle for several minutes on the hangman's noose before he died. Bryce is said to have been an uncle to James Bryce, also executed at Edinburgh in 1844 for the murder of a brother-in-law. (D.1864/685.4/439)

From 1856, the particulars to be entered in the register of deaths were as follows.

(1) The surname, Christian names, and rank, profession or occupation of the deceased and whether single, married or widowed, along with the names of any spouses. If the surname had been changed, then both names were to be stated, e.g. "Hamilton (formerly Bruce)".

(2) The year, day of the month and hour when the death took place and the name of the place. This information might not always be certain, as in the case of a man dying alone in a moving railway carriage. Deaths were registered in the districts where they occurred, irrespective of the place of burial. Some people died in city nursing homes, far from their parish. However, deaths by drowning were registered where the body was found or brought ashore.

(3) The sex of the deceased, male or female.

(4) His or her age. If there was no written proof of age, then the age stated was accepted. Of those born before 1855, ages might not be accurate. Vanity reduces the ages of many people and an informant might have been

Both irregular and regular marriages could be registered as shown by these two very different photographs. The first shows a tinker's wedding at Blairgowrie in Perthshire c.1910. The second (opposite), the marriage of Mary Helen Hay and James Thomson at Ardallie in Aberdeenshire in 1912. (Scottish Life Archive)

44

misinformed. After 1908, some people who had claimed to be over 70 to obtain the old age pension turned out to be younger than 70 when they died a few years later.

(5) The names and rank, profession or occupation of the parents of the deceased. It was not always possible to provide this valuable genealogical information. There might be no one to remember the parents of elderly people, such as those who died in the poorhouse. Even their children might not know. When William Fraser registered the death of his father, James Fraser, labourer, in the parish of Petty in 1864, James's parents

were "Not Known". And children might get it wrong. When James Sinclair, farmer, died in South Ronaldsay in 1870, his son Isaac named his maternal grandmother as his father's mother.

(6) The cause of death. Any medical person in attendance during the last illness was bound to send the registrar a certificate stating the cause. Registrars constantly complained of the illegible writing of such certificates! If no medical practitioner

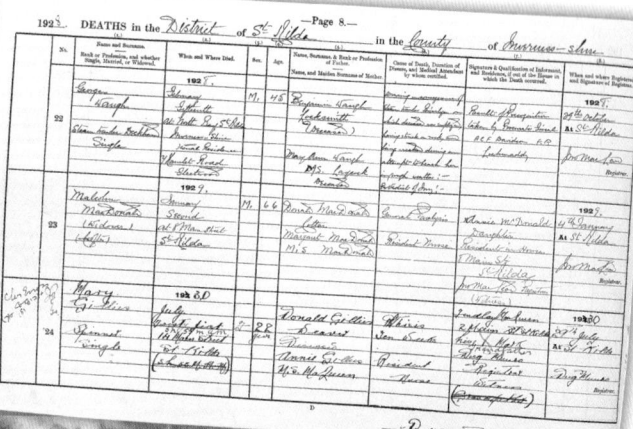

The General Register Office for Scotland records events not just about individuals, but they also reflect the constantly changing pattern of Scottish life through its communities. Here we see the coffin of Mary Gillies who died on St Kilda aged 26 of tuberculosis. She died only 3 weeks before the island was finally evacuated in 1930, and hers is the last death entry ever recorded for that community. (Scottish Life Archive).

46

had been in attendance, as was quite common in the 19th century in rural and poorer urban areas, then the informant might provide the cause of death. This might be simply "old age" or "by the Will of God". In 1857 in Glasgow a registrar noted gleefully that a temperance hotel keeper had died from intemperance. The registrar of Watten in 1860 recorded "accidental death by a pig". As the years progressed, the causes of death were increasingly described in medical terms.

(7) The signature and qualification of the informant, who was usually the nearest relative present at the death, but could be an occupier or inmate of the house where the death occurred. If a dead body was found exposed, then the informant was the person who found it or the public officer to whom the body was brought.

(8) Date of registration and signature of the registrar.

The registrar had to inform the procurator fiscal of any death attended by violence or of which the cause was unexplained. If, on that information or otherwise, a precognition was held on the death, revealing details additional or alternative to those already reported to the registrar, then the procurator fiscal would so inform the registrar who would enter them in his register of corrected entries.

After an entry in a register had been completed, an error might be discovered, especially if there had been a precognition, or other alterations sought. The original entry could not be altered. Instead, each registrar kept a register of corrected entries in which such amendments were written, after they had been approved by a sheriff. A cross reference was noted in the margin of the original entry. Examples of corrections are changes of name, age, residence and even identity (as when a hospital told relatives that the wrong patient had died). Whole entries might be found to be fictitious and require to be cancelled.

Entries in the birth and death registers were usually initiated by an informant visiting the registrar. The procedure for registering marriages was rather different. Before the marriage, the contracting parties had to obtain a schedule, which was completed by the clergyman at the time of the marriage and then brought to the registrar for registration of the marriage. Clergymen of all denominations could now celebrate regular marriages. Some caused problems, by not completing the schedule properly. In the 1850s, Free Church ministers were alleged to be careless in this respect, being openly hostile to the Registration Act, while the Church of Scotland and Roman

Catholic clergy were keen for the new system to work properly. In 1855, one couple got married in Dundee and promptly left for America, taking their schedule with them, so that the marriage could not be registered. A registrar could be invited to attend the wedding, carrying his register (carefully protected from the elements).

Irregular marriages could also be registered, provided their existence had been established by a court of law. This route might be taken by a couple who belonged to a religious sect which did not have an officiating clergyman.

The particulars to be entered in the schedule and in the register of marriages from 1856 were as follows.

(1) Year, day of the month, place and mode of celebration (i.e. according to the forms of whichever Church). In 19th century Scotland marriages rarely took place in a church. The usual location was the bride's home, but hotels also became fashionable. An entry in the Applecross register in 1860 failed to name a place, because "the parties met the minister by the wayside and the marriage was solemnised at a big stone. In a wild country like the West of Scotland this mode of procedure is by no means uncommon." Some people preferred to get married away from home. In 1865, "One half of the Eyemouth marriages are solemnised in Edinburgh where the parties resort to save expense and to be free from annoyance occasioned by the uproar usual at such times." Marriages were registered in the district in which they were solemnised.

(2) Signatures of the parties, their rank, profession or occupation, relationship if related, and condition (bachelor, spinster, widower or widow). Very occasionally these might be inaccurate. Bigamy might occur, and there are proven instances where people married under the name of another. In Dundee in 1855, after the banns had been called, a couple quarrelled. To save the expense of new banns, the man married another woman under the name of the first.

(3) Their ages. Until 1929, the minimum age for marriage was 14 for a man and 12 for a woman. Since 1929, it is 16 for both sexes.

(4) Their usual residences.

(5) Names of their parents and the rank, profession or occupation of their fathers. More valuable genealogical information.

(6) Signature of the officiating minister and at least two witnesses.

(7) Date of registration and signature of the registrar.

Sometimes parties or witnesses or informants had to sign by a mark, in which case that had to be witnessed by two people. The extent of such instances might be a comment on the literacy of a district.

Over the years, registrars acquired additional duties. From 1861, they were required to supervise the taking of the Census in their districts. From 1864, they had to note on birth entries when a child was vaccinated. In 1866 they were required to make returns of epidemic diseases in their districts. From 1878, as an alternative to the proclamation of banns, a notice of intended marriage could be posted outside the registrar's office. They were required at various dates to inform assorted government departments of the death of pensioners and medical bodies of the death of practitioners. From the 1st of July 1940, they were authorised to perform marriage ceremonies.

From the beginning, the registers of births, deaths and marriages could be searched by members of the public, though for particular entries only. Browsing was and is not permitted. Nowadays, researchers may inspect the registers in the General Register Office in Edinburgh, aided by the wonderful computer search mechanism. That would be a perfect system were it not for the contrariness of some of our deceased relatives who altered their names unofficially or who spelt their names variously during life. For total perfection, registration requires continuity and human beings are rarely consistent.

Shipyard workers on the Clyde, c.1907. Despite the seeming anonymity of these workers, ending their day's shift from building the liner 'Lusitania', every individual will be recorded and their memory preserved forever in the records held by the General Register Office for Scotland. (The National Archives of Scotland: UCS1/367/178/5).

Documentary Sources and Publications Used

Old parochial registers, 1553-1854.

Census returns, 1841-1891.

Statutory registers of births, deaths and marriages (from 1855).

Archive files, General Register Office for Scotland (preserved in the National Archives of Scotland (NAS))

- GRO.1 Registration Services
- GRO.4 Establishment Branch
- GRO.5 Registration Branch
- GRO.6 Census Branch

Acts of Parliament concerning registration and census taking.

Sketch of the history and imperfect condition of the parochial records of births, deaths, and marriages in Scotland by George Seton (1854).

Detailed list of the old parochial registers of Scotland (1872).

The statistical account of Scotland compiled by Sir John Sinclair (1791-1799).

The new statistical account of Scotland (1845).

"Genealogical gems"; "A history of registration"; GROS Frequently Asked Questions (FAQs); "New Register House - a living repository" (GROS Internet publications).

Lecture notes by Registrars General and their staff (preserved in the NAS, reference GRO4/33).

Registrar General's private information folders (GROS Library collection).

Printed articles in *The Scottish genealogist* [quarterly journal of the Scottish Genealogy Society (SGS)],
- *Church records*. Lecture to the SGS, Gordon Donaldson (1955).
- *Parish registers in the New Register House*. Lecture to the SGS, E A Hogan, Registrar General (1956).
- *Registration and censuses*, A B Taylor, Registrar General (1962).
- *Recent developments at New Register House*. Lecture to the SGS, A L Rennie, Registrar General (1971).
- *Old Parish Registers*, 1974 conference address to the Institute of Population Registration, D Baird (1974).

Population registration [journal of the Institute of Population Registration]
- *Notes on the old parochial registers of Scotland*, Patricia Baxendine (1974).

and *Genealogists' magazine: the journal of the Society of Genealogists*
- *Some problems with Scottish family history relating to old parish registers*, John Shaw, Departmental Record Officer, GROS (1988).

Scottish population statistics including Webster's analysis of population, 1755 (Scottish History Society, 1952).

The Census: Notes for lessons in schools, Census Office, GROS, 1931.

Published census reports for Scotland, 1841-1891.

Register of Acts of the General Assembly of the Church of Scotland (preserved in the NAS, reference CH1/1).

Hansard (official reports of Parliament), March-May 1854.

Regulations for registrars, 1855-1940 (GROS Library collection).

The encyclopaedia of Scottish executions 1750 to 1963 by Alex F Young (1998).